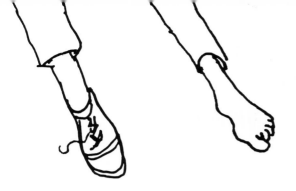

Falling
Up

Falling Up

poems and drawings by

Shel Silverstein

HarperCollins*Publishers*

FALLING UP
Copyright © 1996 by Shel Silverstein

All rights reserved. No part of this book may be used or repro-
duced in any manner whatsoever without written permission
except in the case of brief quotations embodied in critical
articles and reviews. Printed in the United States of America.
For information address HarperCollins Children's Books, a
division of HarperCollins Publishers, Inc., 10 East 53rd Street,
New York, NY 10022.

Book and jacket design by Kim Llewellyn

Production: John Vitale, Lisa Ford
Copyediting: Renée Vera Cafiero
Linotype setting: Louis Lucchi
Research: Seymour Haber
Printing and binding: The Book Press, Brattleboro, VT

Library of Congress Catalog Card Number: 96-75736

ISBN 0-06-024802-5
ISBN 0-06-024803-3 (lib. bdg.)

19 18 17 16 15 14 13 12 11

FALLING UP

I tripped on my shoelace
And I fell up—
Up to the roof tops,
Up over the town,
Up past the tree tops,
Up over the mountains,
Up where the colors
Blend into the sounds.
But it got me so dizzy
When I looked around,
I got sick to my stomach
And I threw down.

PLUGGING IN

Peg plugged in her 'lectric toothbrush,
Mitch plugged in his steel guitar,
Rick plugged in his CD player,
Liz plugged in her VCR.
Mom plugged in her 'lectric blanket,
Pop plugged in the TV fights,
I plugged in my blower-dryer—
Hey! Who turned out all the lights?

COMPLAININ' JACK

This morning my old jack-in-the-box
Popped out—and wouldn't get back-in-the-box.
He cried, "Hey, there's a tack-in-the-box,
And it's cutting me through and through.

"There also is a crack-in-the-box,
And I never find a snack-in-the-box,
And sometimes I hear a quack-in-the-box,
'Cause a duck lives in here too."

Complain, complain is all he did—
I finally had to close the lid.

SUN HAT

Oh, what a sweet child is Hannah Hyde,
Oh, how thoughtful, oh, how nice,
To buy a hat with a brim so wide,
It gives shade to the frogs
And the worms and the mice.

SNOWBALL

I made myself a snowball
As perfect as could be.
I thought I'd keep it as a pet
And let it sleep with me.
I made it some pajamas
And a pillow for its head.
Then last night it ran away,
But first—it wet the bed.

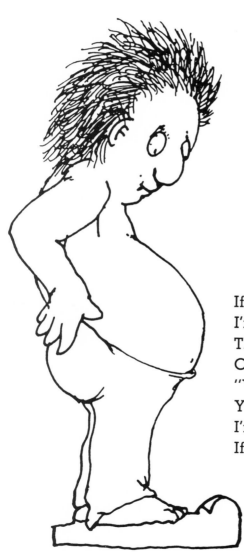

SCALE

If I could only see the scale,
I'm sure that it would state
That I've lost ounces . . . maybe pounds
Or even *tons* of weight.
"You'd better eat some pancakes—
You're skinny as a rail."
I'm sure that's what the scale would say . . .
If I could see the scale.

LITTLE PIG'S TREAT

Said the pig to his pop,
"There's the candy shop.
Oh, please let's go inside.
And I promise I won't
Make a *kid* of myself
If you give me a *people-back* ride."

UNFAIR

They don't allow pets in this apartment.
That's not decent, that's not fair.
They don't allow pets in this apartment.
They don't listen, they don't care.
I told them he's quiet and never does bark,
I told them he'd do all his stuff in the park,
I told them he's cuddly and friendly, and yet—
They won't allow pets.

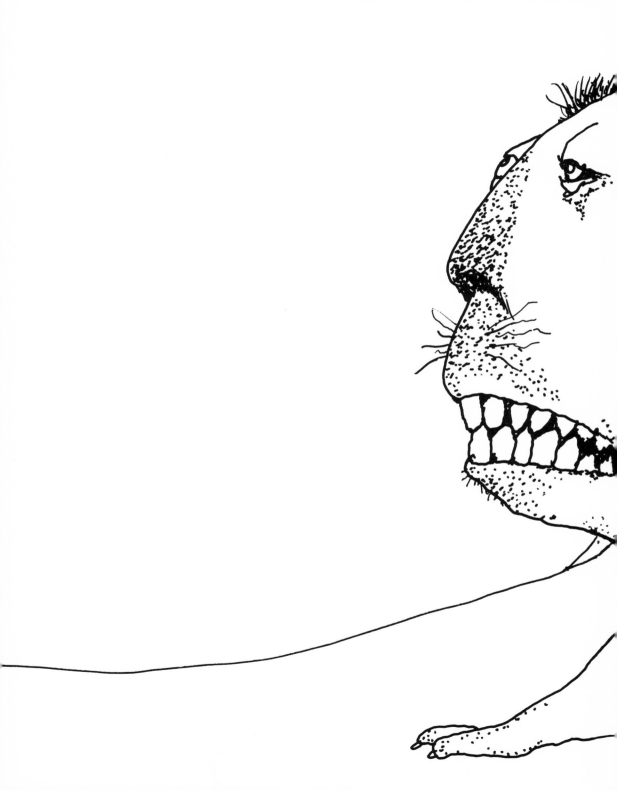

WASTEBASKET BROTHER

Someone put their baby brother
Under this basket—
The question is exactly why,
But I'm not going to ask it.
But someone, I ain't sayin' who,
Has got a guilty face,
Ashamed for lettin' such a lovely brother
Go to waste.

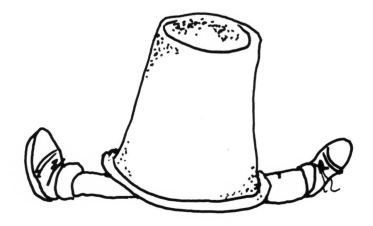

CRYSTAL BALL

Come see your life in my crystal glass—
Twenty-five cents is all you pay.
Let me look into your past—
Here's what you had for lunch today:
Tuna salad and mashed potatoes,
Green pea soup and apple juice,
Collard greens and stewed tomatoes,
Chocolate milk and lemon mousse.
You admit I've told it all?
Well, I know it, I confess,
Not by looking in my ball,
But just by looking at your dress.

ADVICE

William Tell, William Tell,
Take your arrow, grip it well,
There's the apple—aim for the middle—
Oh well . . . you just missed by a *little*.

NOPE

I put a piece of cantaloupe
Underneath the microscope.
I saw a million strange things sleepin',
I saw a zillion weird things creepin',
I saw some green things twist and bend—
I won't eat cantaloupe again.

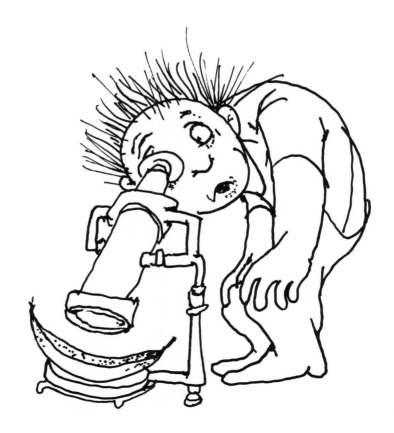

NO THANK YOU

No I do not want a kitten,
No cute, cuddly kitty-poo,
No more long hair in my cornflakes,
No more midnight meowing mews.

No more scratchin', snarlin', spitters,
No more sofas clawed to shreds,
No more smell of kitty litter,
No more mousies in my bed.

No I will not take that kitten—
I've had lice and I've had fleas,
I've been scratched and sprayed and bitten,
I've developed allergies.

If you've got an ape, I'll take him,
If you have a lion, that's fine,
If you brought some walking bacon,
Leave him here, I'll treat him kind.

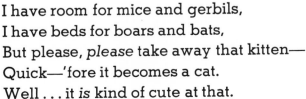

I have room for mice and gerbils,
I have beds for boars and bats,
But please, *please* take away that kitten—
Quick—'fore it becomes a cat.
Well . . . it *is* kind of cute at that.

MORGAN'S CURSE

Followin' the trail on the old treasure map,
I came to the spot that said "Dig right here."
And four feet down my spade struck wood
Just where the map said a chest would appear.
But carved in the side were written these words:
"A curse upon he who disturbs this gold."
Signed, Morgan the Pirate, Scourge of the Seas.
I read these words and my blood ran cold.
So here I sit upon untold wealth
Tryin' to figure which is worse:
How much do I need this gold?
And how much do I need this curse?

WARNING
A CURSE UPON
HE WHO DISTURBS
THIS
GOLD M.

NEEDLES AND PINS

Needles and pins,
Needles and pins,
Sew me a sail
To catch me the wind.

Sew me a sail
Strong as the gale,
Carpenter, bring out your
Hammers and nails.

Hammers and nails,
Hammers and nails,
Build me a boat
To go chasing the whales.

Chasing the whales,
Sailing the blue,
Find me a captain
And sign me a crew.

Captain and crew,
Captain and crew,
Take me, oh take me
To anywhere new.

DIVING BOARD

You've been up on that diving board
Making sure that it's nice and straight.
You've made sure that it's not too slick.
You've made sure it can stand the weight.
You've made sure that the spring is tight.
You've made sure that the cloth won't slip.
You've made sure that it bounces right,
And that your toes can get a grip—
And you've been up there since half past five
Doin' everything . . . but DIVE.

SAFE?

I look to the left,
I look to the right,
Before I ever
Move my feet.
No cars to the left,
No cars to the right,
I guess it's safe
To cross the street. . . .

NOISE DAY

Let's have one day for girls and boyses
When you can make the grandest noises.
Screech, scream, holler, and yell—
Buzz a buzzer, clang a bell,
Sneeze—hiccup—whistle—shout,
Laugh until your lungs wear out,
Toot a whistle, kick a can,
Bang a spoon against a pan,
Sing, yodel, bellow, hum,
Blow a horn, beat a drum,
Rattle a window, slam a door,
Scrape a rake across the floor,

Use a drill, drive a nail,
Turn the hose on the garbage pail,
Shout Yahoo—Hurrah—Hooray,
Turn up the music all the way,
Try and bounce your bowling ball,
Ride a skateboard up the wall,
Chomp your food with a smack and a slurp,
Chew—chomp—hiccup—burp.
One day a year do *all* of these,
The rest of the days—be *quiet* please.

MY SNEAKY COUSIN

She put in her clothes,
Then thought she'd get
A free bath here
At the launderette.
So round she goes now,
Flippity-flappy,
Lookin' clean—
But not too happy.

28

LITTLE HOARSE

My voice was raspy, rough, and cracked.
I said, "I am a little hoarse."
They stuck a saddle on my back
And jumped on me—and now, of course,
They trot me and they gallop me,
They prance me up and down the town
Yellin', "Giddy up, little hoarse."
(Some things don't mean the way they sound.)

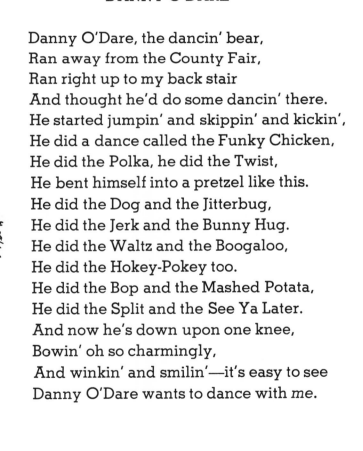

DANNY O'DARE

Danny O'Dare, the dancin' bear,
Ran away from the County Fair,
Ran right up to my back stair
And thought he'd do some dancin' there.
He started jumpin' and skippin' and kickin',
He did a dance called the Funky Chicken,
He did the Polka, he did the Twist,
He bent himself into a pretzel like this.
He did the Dog and the Jitterbug,
He did the Jerk and the Bunny Hug.
He did the Waltz and the Boogaloo,
He did the Hokey-Pokey too.
He did the Bop and the Mashed Potata,
He did the Split and the See Ya Later.
And now he's down upon one knee,
Bowin' oh so charmingly,
And winkin' and smilin'—it's easy to see
Danny O'Dare wants to dance with *me*.

FURNITURE BASH

The hand of the clock
Pinched the foot of the bed,
So the foot of the bed
Kicked the seat of the chair,
So the seat of the chair
Sat on the head of the table,
So the head of the table
Bit the leg of the desk,
So the leg of the desk
Bumped the arm of the couch,
So the arm of the couch
Slapped the face of the clock.
And they pinched and they punched
And they banged and they knocked,
And they ripped and they flipped,
And they rolled and they rocked,
And the poor dresser drawer
Got a couple of socks.
There was sawdust and springs
When I turned on the light
After that horrible furniture fight.

And that's the truth, no lie—no joke.
That's how your furniture
All got broke.

WHY IS IT?

Why is it some mornings
Your clothes just don't fit?
Your pants are too short
To bend over or sit,
Your sleeves are too long
And your hat is too tight—
Why is it some mornings
Your clothes don't feel right?

TURKEY?

I only ate one drumstick
At the picnic dance this summer,
Just one little drumstick—
They say I couldn't be dumber.
One tough and skinny drumstick,
Why was that such a bummer?
But everybody's mad at me,
Especially the drummer.

LONG-LEG LOU
AND SHORT-LEG SUE

Long-Leg Lou and Short-Leg Sue
Went for a walk down the avenue,
Laughin' and jokin' like good friends do,
Long-Leg Lou and Short-Leg Sue.

Says Long-Leg Lou to Short-Leg Sue,
"Can't you walk faster than you do?
It really drives me out of my mind
That I'm always in front, and you're always behind."

Says Short-Leg Sue to Long-Leg Lou,
"I walk as fast as I'm meant to do."
"Then I'll go walkin' with someone new,"
Says Long-Leg Lou to Short-Leg Sue.

Now Long-Leg Lou, he walks alone,
Looking for someone with legs like his own,
And sometimes he thinks of those warm afternoons
Back when he went walkin' with Short-Leg Sue.

And Short-Leg Sue strolls down the street
Hand in hand with Slow-Foot Pete,
And they take small steps and they do just fine,
And no one's in front and no one's behind.

MY ROBOT

I told my robot to do my biddin'.
He yawned and said, "You must be kiddin'."
I told my robot to cook me a stew.
He said, "I got better things to do."
I told my robot to sweep my shack.
He said, "You want me to strain my back?"
I told my robot to answer the phone.
He said, "I must make some calls of my own."
I told my robot to brew me some tea.
He said, "Why don't you make tea for me?"
I told my robot to boil me an egg.
He said, "First—lemme hear you beg."
I told my robot, "There's a song you can play me."
He said, "How much are you gonna pay me?"
So I sold that robot, 'cause I never knew
Exactly who belonged to *who*.

THE DEADLY EYE

It's the deadly eye
Of Poogley-Pie.
Look away, look away,
As you walk by,
'Cause whoever looks right at it
Surely will die.
It's a good thing you *didn't* . . .
You did? . . .
Good-bye.

THE VOICE

There is a voice inside of you
That whispers all day long,
"I feel that this is right for me,
I know that *this* is wrong."
No teacher, preacher, parent, friend
Or wise man can decide
What's right for you—just listen to
The voice that speaks inside.

MARI-LOU'S RIDE

The swing swang
The ropes snapped
The seat sailed
And she flew.

Her heart sang
Her shirt flapped
Her coat tailed
Her hair blew.

The bells rang
The crowd clapped
Her mom wailed
And wept too.

Then crash—bang
Into her lap
By air mail
Came Mari-Lou.

THE MONKEY

1 little monkey
Was goin' 2 the store
When he saw a banana 3
He'd never climbed be 4.
By 5 o'clock that evenin'
He was 6 with a stomach ache
'Cause 7 green bananas
Was what that monkey 8.

By 9 o'clock that evenin'
That monkey was quite ill,
So 10 we called the doctor
Who was 11 on the hill.
The doctor said, "You're almost dead.
Don't eat green bananas no more."
The sick little monkey groaned and said,
"But *that's* what I 1-2 the 3-4."

IMAGING

You're only just *imagining*
A mouse is in your hair.
You've got to stop imagining
That mice are everywhere.
I think you're just imagining
To give yourself a scare,
But trust me dear, I wouldn't lie:
There is *no* mouse up there.

41

CEREAL

Rice Krispies stay crisp, though they now and then lisp
As they whisper their "thnap crackle pop" in your bowl,
And though you pour a tall can
Of milk on your All Bran,
It never will turn into glop (so I'm told).

I know Shredded Wheat will stay crumbly and neat
Though you soak it a year in the depths of the ocean,
And from breakfast to lunch
Your Post Toasties will crunch
To show you their love and undying devotion.

Oaties stay oaty, and Wheat Chex stay floaty,
And nothing can take the puff out of Puffed Rice.
But I wish they'd invent a cereal for someone
Who likes it
                All floppy
                And drippy
                And droopy
                And lumpy
                And sloppy
                And soggy
                And gloopy
                And gooey
                And mushy
                And NICE!

SIDEWALKING

They say if you step on a crack,
You will break your mother's back.
But that's just silly, ha-ha-ha—
*Oops—Plop—*Sorry, Ma.

SCREAMIN' MILLIE

Millie McDeevit screamed a scream
So loud it made her eyebrows steam.
She screamed so loud her jawbone broke,
Her tongue caught fire, her nostrils smoked,
Her eyeballs boiled and then popped out,
Her ears flew north, her nose went south,
Her teeth flew out, her voice was wrecked,
Her head went sailing off her neck—
Over the hillside, 'cross the stream,
Into the skies it chased the scream.
And that's what happened to Millie McDeevit
(At least I hope all you screamers believe it).

TATTOOIN' RUTH

Collars are choking,
Pants are expensive,
Jackets are itchy and hot,
So tattooin' Ruth tattooed me a suit.
Now folks think I'm *dressed*—
When I'm not.

PINOCCHIO

Pinocchio, Pinocchio,
That little wooden bloke-io,
His nose, it grew an inch or two
With every lie he spoke-io.

Pinocchio, Pinocchio,
Thought life was just a joke-io,
'Til the mornin' that he met that cat
And the fox in a long red cloak-io.

They cried, "Come on, Pinocchio,
We'll entertain the folk-io,
On puppet strings you'll dance and sing
From Timbuktu to Tokyo."

Pinocchio, Pinocchio,
Got sold to a trav'lin' show-kio,
Got put in a cage by a man in a rage
With a stick to give him a poke-io.

So Pinocchio, Pinocchio,
Out of that cage he broke-io
To the land where boys just play with toys
And cuss and fight and smoke-io.

Pinocchio, Pinocchio,
He finally awoke-io
With donkey ears and little-boy tears,
And his poor wooden heart was broke-io.

So back home ran Pinocchio
As fast as he could go-kio,
But his daddy, he had gone to sea,
So off to sea went Pinocchio.

Pinocchio, Pinocchio,
He got quite a soak-io
When he lost his sail and got ate by a whale,
And it looked like he was gonna croak-io.

But Pinocchio, Pinocchio,
A fire he did stoke-io
Inside that whale, who sneezed up a gale
And blew him out in the smoke-io.

Pinocchio, Pinocchio,
Next mornin' he awoke-io,
And he had no strings or puppety things,
And his donkey ears had disappeared,

E 9 LIE 10 LIE 11 LIE 12 LIE 13 LIE 14

And his nose—surprise—was the normal size,
And his body felt fine, not made of pine,
And he cried, "Oh joy, I'm a real boy,
And everything's okey-dokey-o."

WEIRD-BIRD

Birds are flyin' south for winter.
Here's the Weird-Bird headin' north,
Wings a-flappin', beak a-chatterin',
Cold head bobbin' back 'n' forth.
He says, "It's not that I like ice
Or freezin' winds and snowy ground.
It's just sometimes it's kind of nice
To be the only bird in town."

STONE AIRPLANE

I made an airplane out of stone . . .
I always did like staying home.

SHARING

I'll share your toys, I'll share your money,
I'll share your toast, I'll share your honey,
I'll share your milk and your cookies too—
The hard part's sharing mine with you.

ICE CREAM STOP

The circus train made an ice cream stop
At the fifty-two-flavor ice cream stand.
The animals all got off the train
And walked right up to the ice cream man.
"I'll take Vanilla," yelled the gorilla.
"I'll take Chocolate," shouted the ocelot.
    "I'll take the Strawberry," chirped the canary.
        "Rocky Road," croaked the toad.
            "Lemon and Lime," growled the lion.
        Said the ice cream man, " 'Til I see a dime,
    You'll get no ice cream of mine."
Then the animals snarled and screeched and growled
And whinnied and whimpered and hooted and howled
And gobbled up the whole ice cream stand,
All fifty-two flavors
(Fifty-*three* with Ice Cream Man).

BIG EATING CONTEST

The entrance fee cost me
Two dollars, and then
It cost twenty more
For those burgers and fries.
My hospital bill
Was a hundred and ten.
But I *won*—
The *five-dollar* first prize!

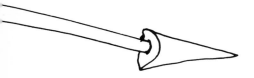

WEB-FOOT WOE

Us swans and geese
Have rotten luck.
You folks don't know
Whose name is whose.
I waddle in—
You all yell, *"Duck."*
Can't you see
That I'm a *goose*?

DON THE DRAGON'S BIRTHDAY

Here he comes across the lake.
He's comin' for his birthday cake.
Sing "Happy Birthday, Dragon Don,"
And watch him blow the candles . . . on.

THE BEAR, THE FIRE, AND THE SNOW

"I live in fear of the snow," said the bear.
"Whenever it's here, be sure I'll be there.
Oh, the pain and the cold,
When one's bearish and old.
I live in fear of the snow."

"I live in fear of the fire," said the snow.
"Whenever it comes then it's time I must go.
With its yellow lick flames
Leaping higher and higher,
I live in fear of the fire."

"I live in fear of the river," said the fire.
"It can drown all my flames anytime it desires,
And the thought of the wet
Makes me sputter and shiver.
I live in fear of the river."

"I live in fear of the bear," said the river.
"It can lap me right up, don't you know?"
While a mile away
You can hear the bear say,
"I live in fear of the snow."

FOOT REPAIR

I walked so much I wore down my feet—
Do you know how weird that feels?
I went to the cobbler. "Aha," says he,
"You need new soles and heels."

So he took some tacks
And some thick new skin,
And quick as quick could be,
He stitched and he clipped
And he glued and he snipped,
And he shined 'em up for me.

But when he said, "Ten dollars, please,"
It almost knocked me flat.
"Ten dollars? Just for heels and soles?
I could have bought new *feet* for that."

WRITER WAITING

Oh this shiny new computer—
There just isn't nothin' cuter.
It knows everything the world ever knew.
And with this great computer
I don't need no writin' tutor,
'Cause there ain't a single thing that it can't do.
It can sort and it can spell,
It can punctuate as well.
It can find and file and underline and type.
It can edit and select,
It can copy and correct,
So I'll have a whole book written by tonight
(Just as soon as it can think of *what* to write).

WARMHEARTED

Beatrice Bright is for animal rights—
She's waiting for Animal Day to arrive.
 And though you see her in her new fox fur,
The fox that she wears is *alive*.

STUPID PENCIL MAKER

Some dummy built this pencil wrong—
The eraser's down here where the point belongs.
And the point's at the top—so it's no good to me.
Its amazing how stupid some people can be.

BAD COLD

This cold is too much for my shirtsleeve.
Go get me a Kleenex—and *fast*.
I sniffle and wheeze
And I'm ready to sneeze
And I don't know how long I can last. . . .

Atchoo—it's too wet for a Kleenex,
So bring me a handkerchief, quick.
It's—a*tchoo*—no joke,
Now the handkerchief's soaked.
Hey, a dish towel just might do the trick.

Atchoo—it's too much for a *bath* towel.
There never has been such a cold.
I'll be better off
With that big tablecloth,
No—bring me the flag off the pole.

Atchoo—bring the clothes from the closet,
Atchaa—get the sheets from the bed,
The drapes off the window,
The rugs off the floor
To soak up this cold in my head.

Atchoo—hurry down to the circus
And ask if they'll lend you the tent.
You say they said yes?
Here it comes—Lord be blessed—
Here it *is*—Ah-kachoooo—there it went.

NEW WORLD

Upside-down trees swingin' free,
Busses float and buildings dangle:
Now and then it's nice to see
The world—from a different angle.

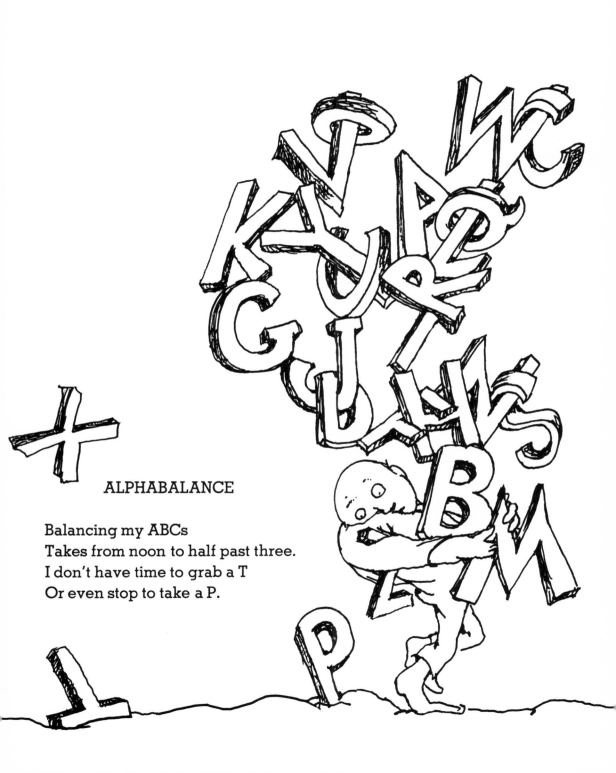

ALPHABALANCE

Balancing my ABCs
Takes from noon to half past three.
I don't have time to grab a T
Or even stop to take a P.

STRANGE RESTAURANT

I said, "I'll take the T-bone steak."
A soft voice mooed, "Oh, wow."
And I looked up and realized
The waitress was a cow.

I cried, "*Mistake*—forget the steak.
I'll take the chicken then."
I heard a cluck—'twas just my luck
The busboy was a *hen*.

I said, "Okay, no fowl today.
I'll have the seafood dish."
Then I saw through the kitchen door
The cook—he was a fish.

I screamed, "Is there anyone workin' here
Who's an onion or a beet?
No? You're *sure*? Okay then, friends,
A salad's what I'll eat."

They looked at me. "Oh, no," they said,
"The owner is a cabbage head."

WOULDA-COULDA-SHOULDA

All the Woulda-Coulda-Shouldas
Layin' in the sun,
Talkin' 'bout the things
They woulda-coulda-shoulda done . . .
But those Woulda-Coulda-Shouldas
All ran away and hid
From one little *did*.

SYBIL THE MAGICIAN'S LAST SHOW

Magical Sybil was much too cheap
To buy her rabbit a carrot.
He grew so thin, just bones and skin,
So starved he couldn't bear it—
And so, as she reached into her hat
To grab him by the ears,
She felt a tug, she felt a pull,
And *WHAP*—she disappeared,
"The greatest act we've ever seen,"
We cheered for Magical Sybil.
But all that remained was a hat and a cape
And the sound of a bunny
Goin', "Nibble . . . nibble . . . nibble."

ROTTEN CONVENTION

They had a Rotten Convention
And everyone was there:
Hamburger Face and Gruesome Grace
And the Skull with the slimy hair.

There was Mr. Mud and the Creepin' Crud
And the Drooler and Belchin' Bob,
There was Three-Headed Ann—she was holdin' hands
With the Whimperin' Simperin' Slob.

The Unpronounceable Name, he came,
And so did Saw-Nose Dan
And Poopin' Pete and Smelly Feet
And the Half-Invisible Man.

There was Sudden Death and Sweat-Sock Breath,
Big Barf and the Deadly Bore,
And Killin' Dillon and other villains
We'd never seen before.

And we all sat around and told bad tales
Of the rottenest people we knew,
And everybody there kept askin' . . .
Where were you?

GARDENER

We gave you a chance
To water the plants.
We didn't mean *that* way—
Now zip up your pants.

MEDUSA

Coil and hiss—writhe and twist—
My hairdo won't get done.
'Cause one hair's hissing, "Ponytail,"
And one yells, "Simple bun."
One whispers, "Cornrows,"
One screams, "Bangs."
One shouts, "Just wash and dry it."
One snaps, "No, curl and tie it,"
One hollers, "Bleach and dye it."
And how am I to fix my hair
If my hair will not keep quiet?

WE'RE OUT OF PAINT, SO . . .

Let's paint a picture with our food.
For red we'll squeeze these cherries.
For purple let's splash grape juice on.
For blue we'll use blueberries.
For black just use some licorice.
For brown pour on some gravy.
For yellow you can dip your brush
In the egg yolk you just gave me.
We'll sign our names in applesauce
And title it "Our Luncheon,"
And hang it up for everyone
To stop . . . and see . . . and *munch* on.

THE GNOME, THE GNAT, AND THE GNU

I saw an ol' gnome
Take a gknock at a gnat
Who was gnibbling the gnose of his gnu.
I said, "Gnasty gnome,
Gnow, stop doing that.
That gnat ain't done gnothing to you."

He gnodded his gnarled ol' head and said,
"'Til gnow I gnever gnew
That gknocking a gnat
In the gnoodle like that
Was gnot a gnice thing to do."

HAND HOLDING

Somebody said, "Let's all hold hands,"
So Lee held hands with Jean.
And Jean also held Helen's hand
While *she* held hands with Dean.
Dean's other hand held Sharma Joy's
While she held hands with *Lee*.
So tell me just how did I wind up
Holdin' hands with me?

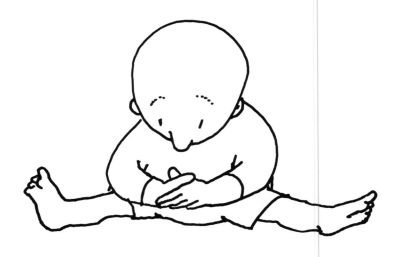

LONG SCARF

You ask me to take off my scarf
And sit down and rest for a while?
That's sweet of you—but before I do,
I'll tell you a story, my child.
Some years ago I fought a duel
With the Count of Doomandread,
And I slipped or tripped
And his sword just clipped
My neck—and sliced off my head.
I scooped it up and put it back,
But it didn't quite connect,
So I tied this scarf around it
Just to keep it on my neck.
That's why I always keep it on,
'Cause if it did unwrap,
This wobbly chopped-off head of mine
Might tumble in your lap.
So now you've heard my tale, and if
It will not make you ill,
And you'd *still* like me to
Take off my scarf . . .
I will!

HARD TO PLEASE
(To be said in one breath)

Elaine gives me a pain,
Gill makes me ill,
Winnie's a ninny,
Orin is borin',
Milly is silly,
Rosy is nosy,
Junie is loony,
Gussie is fussy,
Jackie is wacky,
Tommy is balmy,
Mary is scary,
Tammy is clammy,
Abby is crabby,
Patti is batty,
Mazie is lazy,
Tiny is whiney,
Missy is prissy,
Nicky is picky,
Ricky is tricky,
And almost everyone
Makes me sicky.
(Whew!)

THEY SAY I HAVE...

They say I have my father's nose,
My grandpa's eyes,
My mother's hair.
Could it be that my behind's
The only thing that's really mine?

THE TOY EATER

You don't have to pick up your toys, okay?
You can leave 'em right there on the floor,
So tonight when the Terrible Toy-Eatin' Tookle
Comes tiptoein' in through the crack in the door,
He'll crunch all your soldiers, he'll munch on your trucks,
He'll chew your poor puppets to shreds,
He'll swallow your Big Wheel and slurp up your paints
And bite off your dear dollies' heads.
Then he'll wipe off his lips with the sails of your ship,
And making a burpity noise,
He'll slither away—but hey, that's okay,
You don't have to pick up your toys.

Alliteration

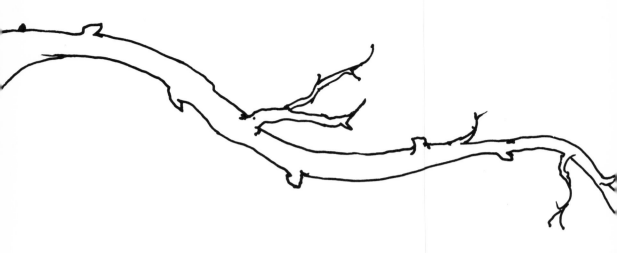

DESCRIPTION

George said, "God is short and fat."
Nick said, "No, He's tall and lean."
Len said, "With a long white beard."
"No," said John, "He's shaven clean."
Will said, "He's black," Bob said, "He's white."
Rhonda Rose said, "He's a *She*."
I smiled but never showed 'em all
The autographed photograph God sent to me.

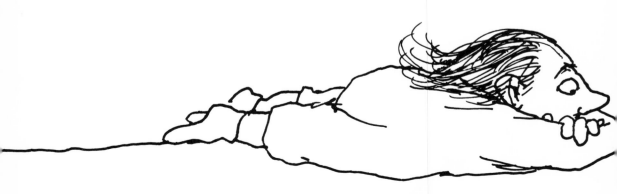

SHOE TALK

There's no one to talk with—
I'll talk with my shoe.
He does have a tongue
And an inner soul, too.
He's awfully well polished,
So straightlaced and neat
(But he talks about *nothing*
But feet—feet—feet).

PEOPLE ZOO

I got grabbed by the elk and the caribou.
They tied me up with a vine lassoo
And whisked me away to Animaloo,
Where they locked me up in the People Zoo.

Now I'm here in a cage that is small as can be
(You can't let wild people just run around free),
And I'm fed bread and tea at a quarter to three,
And the animals all come and gander at me.

They point and they giggle and sometimes they spit
(There's bars on my cage, so they can't poke or hit),
And they scream, "Do a trick," but I stubbornly sit,
Not doin' nothin' . . . but thinkin' a bit.

So if you come visit, just howl, honk, or moo
And try to pretend you're an animal, too,
'Cause if you're a person, they'll throw you into
Cage Two of the zoo here in Animaloo.

THE TONGUE STICKER-OUTER

They say that once in Zanzibar
A boy stuck out his tongue so far,
It reached the heavens and touched a star,
Which burned him rather badly.

I wasn't there, but they say that lout
Now keeps his tongue inside his mouth,
But if you ask him to stick it out . . .
I think he'll do it gladly.

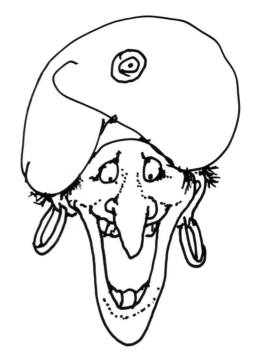

HYPNOTIZED

How would you like to get hypnotized?
Stare deep, deep into my eyes.
Now you're getting drowsy, falling deep
Deep, deep, deep—asleep,
And I have you in my power.
Mow the lawn for half an hour.
Shine my shoes, trim my hair,
Wash out all my underwear.
Do my homework, scratch my back,
Cook me up a great big stack
Of pancakes, and go wash my plate.
Get some nails and fix the gate.
Now wake up and open your eyes.
Wasn't it fun to be hypnotized?

SETTIN' AROUND

Settin' 'round the campfire
With a Werewolf, a Ghoul, and a Vampire,
I told 'em the story of Murderin' Mack,
And the Ghoul ran off screamin'
And never came back.

Settin' 'round the campfire
With the Werewolf and the Vampire,
I told 'em the tale of Three-Headed Ed,
And the Werewolf ran home
And hid under the bed.

Settin' 'round the campfire,
Just me and that ol' Vampire,
I read him the poem of the skeleton bone,
And now it's just me,
Settin' here all alone.

RED FLOWERS FOR YOU

They could be poison ivy,
They might be poison oak,
But anyway, here's your bouquet!
Hey—can't you take a joke?

MY NOSE GARDEN

I have rowses and rowses of noses and noses,
And why they all growses I really can't guess.
No lilies or roses, just cold-catching noses,
And when they all blowses, it's really a mess.

They runs and they glowses, these sneezity noses,
They drips and they flowses, they blooms and they dies.
But you can't bring no noses to fine flower showses
And really expect them to give you a prize.

But each mornin' I goeses to water with hoses
These rowses of noses that I cannot sell,
These red sniffly noses that cause all my woeses,
Why even the crowses complain that they *smell*.

Why noses, not roses? Well, nobody knowses.
Why do you supposes they growses this thick?
But since there's no roses come gather some noses—
I guarantee each one's a good nose to pick.

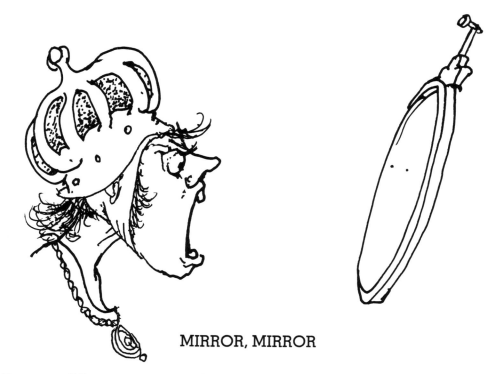

MIRROR, MIRROR

QUEEN: Mirror, mirror on the wall,
          Who is the fairest of them all?

MIRROR: Snow White, Snow White, Snow White—
          I've told you a million times tonight.

QUEEN: Mirror, mirror on the wall,
          What would happen if I let you fall?
          You'd shatter to bits with a clang and a crash,
          Your glass would be splintered—swept out with the trash,
          Your frame would be bent, lying here on the floor—

MIRROR: Hey . . . go ahead, ask me just once more.

QUEEN: Mirror, mirror on the wall,
          Who is the fairest of them all?

MIRROR: *You—you*—It's true,
          The fairest of all is *you—you—you.*
          (*Whew!*)

SPOILED BRAT

The spoiled brat cut a hole in her hat,
The spoiled brat put a coat on the cat,
The spoiled brat got into a spat
'Bout whether a rodent's a mouse or a rat.

The spoiled brat broke a bike with her bat,
The spoiled brat told the policeman to scat,
The spoiled brat said her sister was fat,
And sat on her birthday cake 'til it was flat.

The spoiled brat, she cussed and she spat,
The spoiled brat pulled the wings off a gnat,
The spoiled brat fell into a vat,
Got cooked up for dinner and that was that.

But in spite of the pepper,
The salt and the sage,
The onions and garlic and oil,
Nobody would touch
A bite of that brat
Because she was so spoiled.

OBEDIENT

Teacher said, "You don't obey.
You fidget and twidget
And won't sit down.
So go stand in the corner now
'Til I say you can turn around."
So there I stood 'til it got dark
Without a whimper or a tear,
'Til everybody else went home.
I guess that she forgot me here.
And that was Friday, so I stayed
All through the weekend—bein' good,
And Monday was the first day of
Summer vacation, so I stood
Through hot July and sticky August,
Tryin' to obey her rule.
Stood right there until September,
When—yikes—they closed down the school!
Boarded up the doors and windows,
Moved to a new one way 'cross town.
So here I've stood for forty years
In dark and dust and creaky sounds,
Waiting for her to say, "Turn around."

This might not be just what she meant,
But me—I'm so obedient.

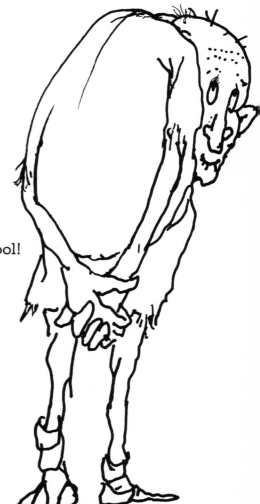

GLUB—GLUB

He thought it was
The biggest puddle
He'd go splashing through.
Turns out it was
The smallest *lake*—
And the *deepest*, too.

GOLDEN GOOSE

Yes, we cooked that fat ol' goose.
You say we were insane
Because she laid those golden eggs,
But you don't know the pain
Of trying to boil a golden egg
While you just starve away.
If she'd laid *ordinary* eggs
She'd be with us today.

REACHIN' RICHARD

'Stead of sayin', "Pass the peas,"
Richard reached across and grabbed some.
'Stead of whisperin', "Lamb chop, please,"
Richard poked his fork and stabbed one.
'Spite his father's warnin' words,
'Spite his mother's tearful teachin',
With each grab his arm did grow
'Til it stretched twenty yards or so.
Said Richard, "Yes, it's weird, I know,
But boy, it's great for reachin'."

HAUNTED

I dare you all to go into
The Haunted House on Howlin' Hill,
Where squiggly things with yellow eyes
Peek past the wormy window sill.
We'll creep into the moonlit yard,
Where weeds reach out like fingers,
And through the rotted old front door
A-squeakin' on its hinges,
Down the dark and whisperin' hall,
Past the musty study,
Up the windin' staircase—
Don't step on the step that's bloody—
Through the secret panel
To the bedroom where we'll slide in
To the ragged cobweb dusty bed
Ten people must have died in.
And the bats will screech,
And the spirits will scream,
And the thunder will crash
Like a horrible dream,
And we'll sing with the zombies
And dance with the dead,
And howl at the ghost
With the axe in his head,
And—come to think of it what do you say
We go get some ice cream instead?

MISTER MOODY

And here we see ol' Mister Moody,
Wearing such a gloomy frown.
But turn him upside down and see . . .

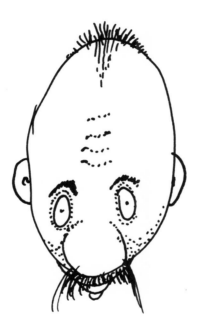

Mister Moody
Upside down—
What did you expect?

EVERY LUNCHTIME

I open my lunch box
Hopin' to find
A sandwich, an apple,
Some cookies or cake.
But there, coiled and hissin',
And set to unwind,
Is another big venomous,
Poisonous snake,
Slitherin' and squirmin'
And hissin' away,
Leavin' me hungry as can be.
It happens every single day...
You think my mother's mad at me?

KANGA RUBY

Hop, nibble, nibble and hop,
What else can you do
But chew that wattle tree bottom to top
When you're a *kangaroo*?

You live down in the dusty bush
Far from the traffic's zoom
With twenty other kangaroos
In one little *kangaroom*....

And when you feel like dancin',
You simply shake a hoof
And hop on the top of your little hut
On your leafy *kangaroof*....

But other times you do wake up
In a mean and nasty mood
And yell at everyone around—
That's really *kangarude*.

No kangaroo hops high as you,
No kangaroo looks cooler,
So they've elected you their queen—
Now you're a *kangaruler*.

And they baked you a queenly cake
Last Wednesday afternoon.
Of course, you went and hopped in it,
And now it's *kangaruined*!

ALLISON BEALS AND HER 25 EELS

Allison Beals had twenty-five eels—
She used four for skateboard wheels,
She used one as a hula hoop,
She used one to stir her soup,
Two of them with silly faces
She would use for sneaker laces,
One was a band to tie her hair,
Two were earrings danglin' there,
One was a ring upon her hand,
One made a perfect wristwatch band,
One of them held her cup of tea,
One held the bandage on her knee,
One was a belt for her cut-off jeans,
One held up her magazines,
One was a necklace that never would choke,
One was a bra strap in case hers broke,
One was a wobbly baton to twirl,
One held a banner that she could unfurl,
One was a bracelet that wouldn't unwind,
One made a lovely Valentine,
The 'lectric one was a lamp that could shine,
And one got a new job on page fifty-nine.

A BATTLE IN THE SKY

It wasn't quite day and it wasn't quite night,
'Cause the sun and the moon were both in sight,
A situation quite all right
With everyone else but them.

So they both made remarks about who gave more light
And who was the brightest and prettiest sight,
And the sun gave a bump and the moon gave a bite,
And the terrible sky fight began.

With a scorch and a sizzle, a screech and a shout,
Across the great heavens they tumbled about,
And the moon had a piece of the sun in its mouth,
While the sun burned the face of the moon.

And when it was over the moon was rubbed red,
And the sun had a very bad lump on its head,
And all the next night the moon stayed home in bed,
And the sun didn't come out 'til noon.

SHORT KID

They said I'd grow another foot
Before I reached the age of ten.
It's true, I grew another foot—
Guess *this* is what they meant.

THE MUMMY

Wrapped myself in toilet paper,
Head to toe to tummy.
Wrapped myself in toilet paper,
Thought that I'd be funny.
Wrapped myself in toilet paper,
Thought they'd call me "Mummy."
Wrapped myself in toilet paper,
They just call me dummy.

SHANNA IN THE SAUNA

"Come into the sauna."
  "No thank you, I don't wanna."
"There's an iguana in the sauna. . . ."
  "I still don't wanna."
"There's a piranha in the sauna. . . ."
  "Now I *really* don't wanna."
"OK, the iguana just ate the piranha,
And the shark just ate the iguana,
So now you can come into the sauna."
  "Now I'm *never* gonna."

A CAT, A KID, AND A MOM

"Why can't you see I'm a cat," said the cat,
"And that's all I ever will be?
Why are you shocked when I roam out at night?
Why are you sad when I meow and I fight?
Why are you sick when I eat up a rat?
I'm a cat."

"Why can't you see I'm a kid?" said the kid.
"Why try to make me like you?
Why are you hurt when I don't want to cuddle?
Why do you sigh when I splash through a puddle?
Why do you scream when I do what I did?
I'm a kid."

"Why can't you see I'm a mom?" said the mom.
"Why try to make me wise?
Why try to teach me the ways of the cat?
Why try to tell me that 'kids are like that'?
Why try to make me be patient and calm?
I'm a mom."

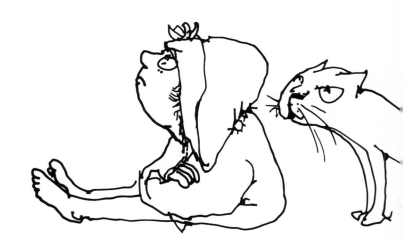

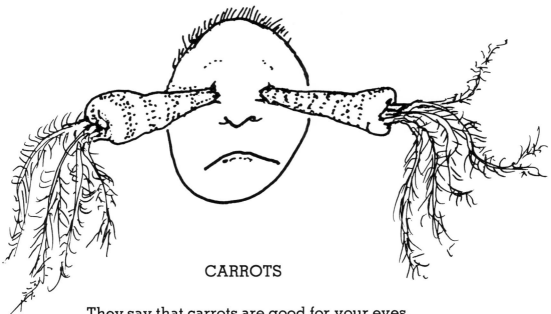

CARROTS

They say that carrots are good for your eyes,
They swear that they improve your sight,
But I'm seein' worse than I did last night—
You think maybe I ain't usin' 'em right?

FEEDING TIME

Oh alligator, palligator, get up out of bed.
It's breakfast time and I can't find
Our keeper Mister Fred.
He smokes a pipe and wears a little
Derby on his head,
And he was 'sposed to meet me here
To help to get you fed.

DANCIN' IN THE RAIN

So what if it drizzles
And dribbles and drips?
I'll splash in the garden,
I'll dance on the roof.
Let it rain on my skin,
It can't get in—
I'm waterproof.

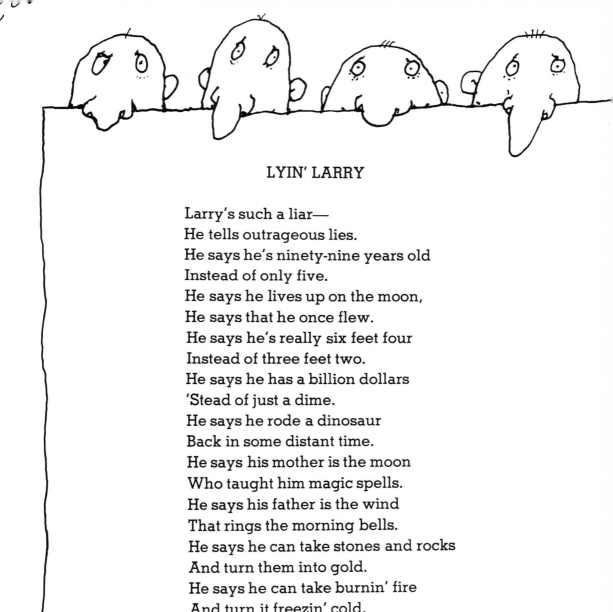

LYIN' LARRY

Larry's such a liar—
He tells outrageous lies.
He says he's ninety-nine years old
Instead of only five.
He says he lives up on the moon,
He says that he once flew.
He says he's really six feet four
Instead of three feet two.
He says he has a billion dollars
'Stead of just a dime.
He says he rode a dinosaur
Back in some distant time.
He says his mother is the moon
Who taught him magic spells.
He says his father is the wind
That rings the morning bells.
He says he can take stones and rocks
And turn them into gold.
He says he can take burnin' fire
And turn it freezin' cold.
He said he'd send me seven elves
To help me with my chores.
But Larry's such a liar—
He only sent me *four*.

THE RUNNERS

Why does our track team run so fast
And jump with zest and zeal?
We owe it all to our great coach
And our wonderful practice field.

REMOTE-A-DAD

It's just like a TV remote control,
Except that it works on fathers.
You just push the thing that you want him to do
And he does it—without any bother.
You want him to dance? Push number five.
You want him to sing? Push seven.
You want him to raise your allowance a bit?
You simply push eleven.
You want him quiet? Just hit Mute.
Fourteen will make him cough.
You want him to stop picking on you?
Yelling and telling you what not to do?
And stop bossing you for an hour or two?
Just push Power—Off.

NO GROWN-UPS

No grown-ups allowed.
We're playin' a game,
And we don't need
"Be-carefuls" or "don'ts."
No grown-ups allowed.
We're formin' a club,
And the secret oath
Must not be shown.
No grown-ups allowed.
We're goin' out for pizza—
No, no one but me and my crowd.
So just stay away.
Oh, now it's time to *pay*?
Grown-ups *allowed.*

THE PORKY

Oh who will wash the porky's ears,
And who will comb his tail,
And who will shine his long sharp quills
And manicure his nails?

Oh Willie may wash the porky's ears,
And Carole may comb his tail,
And Sidney may shine his long sharp quills,
And I'll go down for the mail. . . .

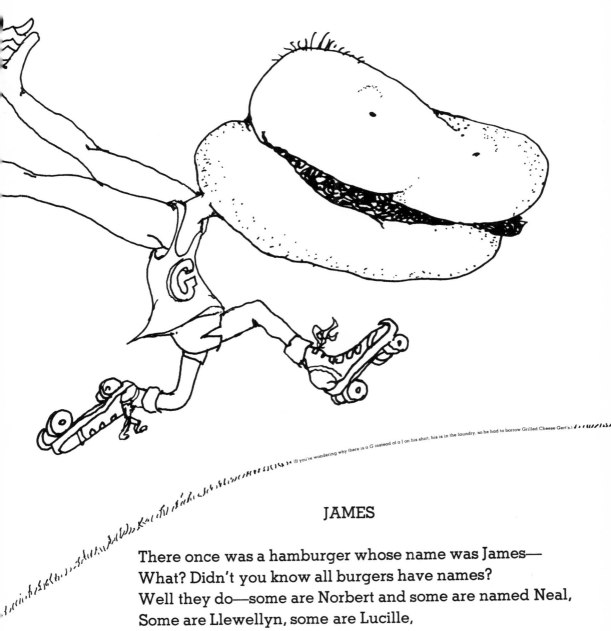

(If you're wondering why there is a G instead of a J on his shirt, his is in the laundry, so he had to borrow Grilled Cheese Gert's.)

JAMES

There once was a hamburger whose name was James—
What? Didn't you know all burgers have names?
Well they do—some are Norbert and some are named Neal,
Some are Llewellyn, some are Lucille,
Some just have nicknames like Bunky or Bean,
Others have long names like Rose-Mavoureen,
Like you, each one's special and no one's the same,
So please, 'fore you bite,
Be polite—ask their name.

SHOW FISH

I found a flounder and I thought, "*Swell,*
I'll take it to school for show and tell."
But I forgot, for quite a spell,
To take it to school for show and tell,
And now it's two weeks later.... Well ...
I'll take it to school for show and *smell*.

NO
No smoking
No spitting
No loitering
No littering
No drinking
No eating
No parking
No speeding
No fishing
No floating
No swimming
No boating
No surfing
No hiking
No hunting
No biking
No running
No skipping
No skinny-dipping
No volleyball players
No spray can sprayers
No fly rod casters
No boom box blasters
No trash leavers
No frisbee heavers
HEY—IT DIDN'T SAY NO BEAVERS.

A CLOSET FULL OF SHOES

Party shoes with frills and bows,
Workin' shoes with steel toes,
Sneakers, flip-flops, and galoshes,
Boots to wear with mackintoshes,
Brogans, oxfords, satin pumps,
Dancin' taps and wooden clumps,
Shoes for climbin', shoes for hikes,
Football cleats and baseball spikes,
Shoes of shiny patent leather,
Woolly shoes for winter weather,
Loafers, rough-outs, sandals, spats,
High heels, low heels, platforms, flats,
Moccasins and fins and flippers,
Shower clogs and ballet slippers . . .
A zillion shoes and just one missin'—
That's the one that matches this'n.

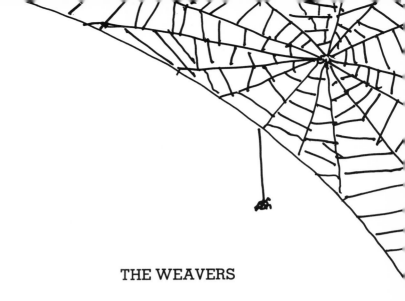

THE WEAVERS

I was sittin', I was knittin'
On a sweater I could wear.
When I finished, I said proudly,
"Hey, I've done some weavin' there."
But ol' spider on the wall said,
"Can you do it in the air?
Can you spin it out of gossamer
From the ceiling to the stair?
Can you let the wind blow through it
So it sways but doesn't tear?
Then can you grab onto it
And swing lightly on a hair?
When you can—then you may truly say,
'I've done some weavin' there.'"

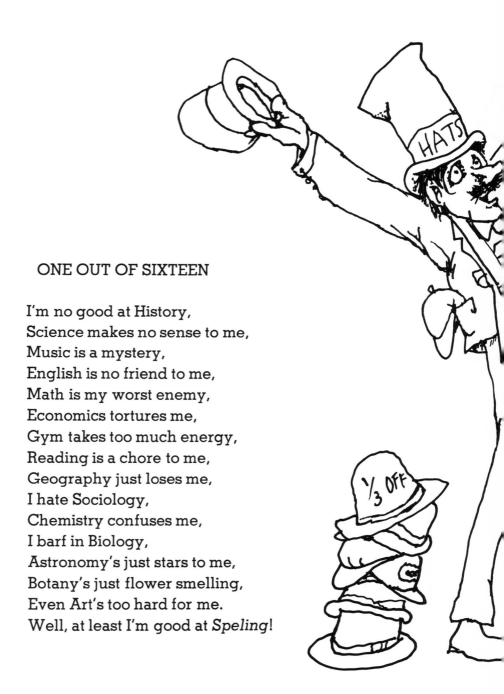

ONE OUT OF SIXTEEN

I'm no good at History,
Science makes no sense to me,
Music is a mystery,
English is no friend to me,
Math is my worst enemy,
Economics tortures me,
Gym takes too much energy,
Reading is a chore to me,
Geography just loses me,
I hate Sociology,
Chemistry confuses me,
I barf in Biology,
Astronomy's just stars to me,
Botany's just flower smelling,
Even Art's too hard for me.
Well, at least I'm good at *Speling*!

HEADLESS TOWN

Selling hats in Headless Town—
Special sale, so gather 'round.
Short brim, wide brim, white or brown,
Hats for sale—in Headless Town.

Selling hats in Headless Town—
Stetson, bonnet, cap, or crown,
Isn't there one soul around
Who needs a hat in Headless Town?

Selling hats in Headless Town
Sure can get a fella down,
But there's a way
If there's a will
(I once sold shoes
In Footlessville).

FORGETFUL PAUL REVERE

Was it *two* if by land
And *one* if by sea?
Or *one* if by land
And *none* if by sea?
Or *none* if by land . . .
Or was it *three*?
My memory's not
What it used to be,
And it's getting so foggy
I hardly can see,
And this hard, cold saddle
Is killin' me—
Oh, what a ride
This is gonna be.

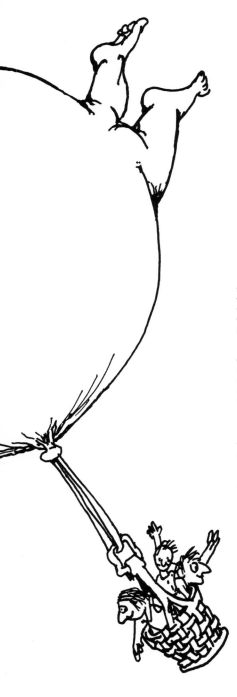

HUMAN BALLOON

Hi-ho for the Human Balloon.
He guzzles up Pepsis and Cokes,
Then gassy and bloaty
And burpy and floaty
He lifts off the ground, while his folks
Hang on to the Human Balloon
As he scoops them right up off the grass,
And as they sail away
They all cheer Hip-Hooray—
And *pray* he don't run out of *gas*.

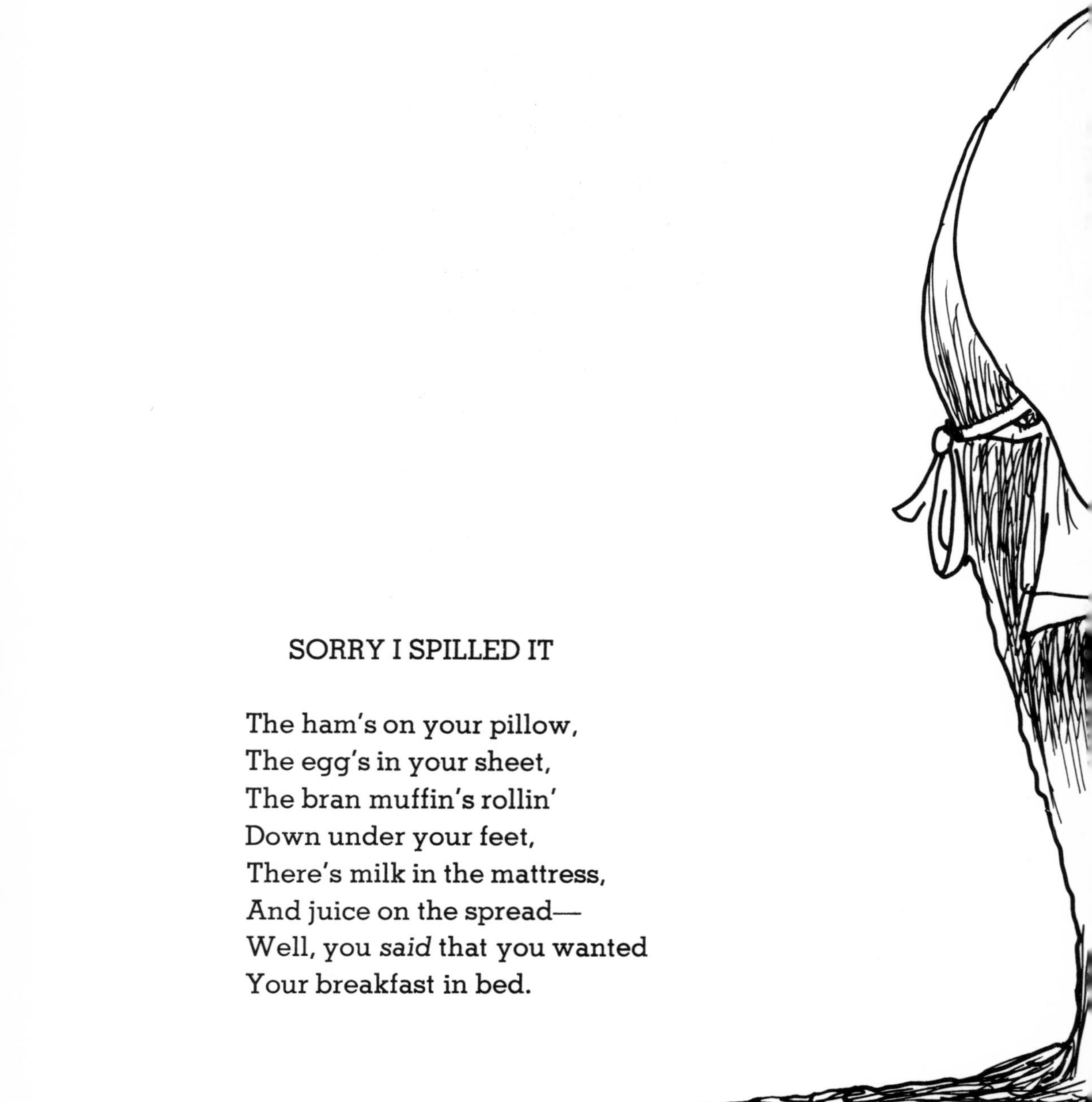

SORRY I SPILLED IT

The ham's on your pillow,
The egg's in your sheet,
The bran muffin's rollin'
Down under your feet,
There's milk in the mattress,
And juice on the spread—
Well, you *said* that you wanted
Your breakfast in bed.

COOKWITCH SANDWICH

I heard that Katrina
The Cook was a witch,
But me, I'm such
A stupid kid,
I yelled, "Hey! Katrina,
Make me a sandwich,"
And ZAP—
She *did!*

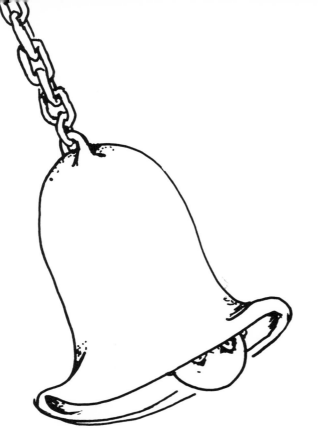

THREE O'CLOCK

I got the job as bell ringer—
DING-DONG—DING-DONG—DING-DONG.
I thought that meant I'd pull the rope—
I—OUCH-OUCH-OUCH—was wrong.

HI-MONSTER

What's that comin'
Through the mist?
The HI-MONSTER—
He's runnin' free.
And if his tail
Is long as this
Just think how *big*
The HI-MONSTER must be.

POISON-TESTER

I'm poison-tester-taster Tru.
I'm here to taste your food for you,
'Cause you could die in half a minute
If there's one drop of *poison* in it.
That lemonade to quench your thirst?
You'd better let me taste it first.
Mmm—it's OK, but these boysenberries—
I'll make sure they're not *poisonberries*.
Mmm—no, they're safe, but that *burger might*
Be deadly—mmm—no, it's all right.
And now I'll test your hot fudge sundae;
Let's hope I'm not dead by Monday.
Mmm—it seems OK, but the poison could be
In the very last bite, so leave it for *me*.
Mmmm—well, it's all safe and my job is through.
See how I risked my life for you?

DENTIST DAN

Nentis Nan, he's my man,
I go do im each chanz I gan.
He sicks me down an creans my teed
Wid mabel syrup, tick an' sweed,
An ten he filks my cavakies
Wid choclut cangy—I tink he's
The graygest nentis in the lan.
Le's hear free jeers for Nentis Nan.
  Pip-pip-ooray!
  Pip-pip-ooray!
  Pip-pip-ooray!
Le's go to Nentis Nan dooday!

KEEPIN' COUNT

Professor Bacar
Keeps flies in a jar
And asks, "Who can tell
Just how many there are?
'Cause whoever can count
The exact right amount
Will get a new bike
And a 'lectric guitar."

So I start tryin',
The flies they start flyin',
I get to three million
And seven, and then—
Some little fly lady
Has one more fly baby,
And I have to go back
And start over again.

CHRISTMAS DOG

Tonight's my first night as a watchdog,
And here it is Christmas Eve.
The children are sleepin' all cozy upstairs,
While I'm guardin' the stockin's and tree.

What's *that* now—footsteps on the rooftop?
Could it be a cat or a mouse?
Who's this down the chimney?
A *thief* with a beard—
And a big sack for robbin' the house?

I'm barkin', I'm growlin', I'm bitin' his butt.
He howls and jumps back in his sleigh.
I scare his strange horses, they leap in the air.
I've frightened the whole bunch away.

Now the house is all peaceful and quiet again,
The stockin's are safe as can be.
Won't the kiddies be glad when they wake up tomorrow
And see how I've guarded the tree.

BITUMINOUS?

The hard coal's called *bituminous*,
Or is that the *anthracite*?
Stalactites grow *down* from caves,
Or do I mean stalag*mites*?
Those fluffy clouds are *nimbus*—
No—wait—they might be *cumulus*.
And that kid who was raised by wolves—
Was he *Remus*—or *Romulus*?
The *brothauruses* ate no meat.
Does that means they're *carnivorous*?
Or were they *brontosauruses*
And were they *herbivorous*?
A camel is a *pachyderm*—
Or do I mean *dromedary*?
Is this match *inflammable*?
I thought it was *incendiary*.
Octagons—no *hexagons*—
No, *heptagons* have seven sides.
And don't spray fruit with pesticides—
Or do I mean *insecticides*?
If I can see right through a thing,
Is it *transparent*—or *translucent*?
These are just *some* of the things
I find confusing . . . or *confuscent*.

MUSIC LESSON

I really should have studied flute,
Harmonica, or chimes.
A clarinet is nice and light,
A fiddle would be fine.
But I had to take piano,
And my teacher is a brute.
He lives up seven flights of stairs.
(I wish I played the flute.)

135

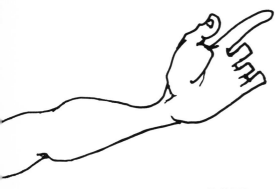

OOH!

I went to the petting zoo-zoo-zoo,
I petted the baby gnu-nu-nu,
I petted the cute cockatoo-too-too,
I petted the kid kangaroo-roo-roo,
I petted the owlet too, too-woo,
I petted the skunklet, too—pee-yoo,
Then I did what one should never do-do-do:
I petted the tigerlet too, ooh—ooh!
Won't somebody please tie my shoe?
Boo—hoo.

CAT JACKS

Do not play jacks
With the Jaguar cat—
You'll never ever beat her.
If she don't win,
She'll start to whine.
If she gets an eight,
She'll pick up nine—
She'll say she didn't,
But you'll know she's lion—
She's such an awful Cheetah.

BLOOD-CURDLING STORY

That story is creepy,
It's waily, it's weepy,
It's screechy and screamy
Right up to the end.
It's spooky, it's crawly,
It's grizzly, it's gory,
It's the *awfulest* story
(Please tell it again).

BEST MASK?

They just had a contest for scariest mask,
And I was the wild and daring one
Who *won* the contest for scariest mask—
And (sob) I'm not even *wearing* one.

THE NAP TAKER

No—I did not take a nap—
The *nap—took—me*
Off the bed and out the window
Far beyond the sea,
To a land where sleepy heads
Read only comic books
And lock their naps in iron safes
So that they can't get took.

And soon as I came to that land,
I also came to grief.
The people pointed at me, shouting,
"Where's the nap, you thief?"
They took me to the courthouse.
The judge put on his cap.
He said, "My child, you are on trial
For taking someone's nap.

"Yes, all you selfish children,
You think just of yourselves
And don't care if the nap you take
Belongs to someone else.
It happens that the nap you took
Without a thought or care
Belongs to Bonnie Bowlingbrook,
Who's sittin' cryin' there.

"She hasn't slept in quite some time—
Just see her eyelids flap.
She's tired and drowsy—cranky too,
'Cause guess who took her nap?"
The jury cried, "You're guilty, yes,
You're guilty as can be,
But just return the nap you took
And we *might* set you free."

"I did not take that nap," I cried,
"I give my solemn vow,
And if I took it by mistake
I do not have it now."
"Oh fiddle-fudge," cried out the judge,
"Your record looks quite sour.
Last night I see you *stole* a kiss,
Last week you *took* a shower,

"You *beat* your eggs, you've *whipped* your cream,
At work you *punched* the clock,
You've even *killed* an hour or two,
We've heard you *darn* your socks,
We know you *shot* a basketball,
You've *stolen* second base,
And we can see you're guilty
From the sleep that's on your face.

"Go lie down on your blanket now
And cry your guilty tears.
I sentence you to one long nap
For ninety million years.
And when the other children see
This nap that never ends,
No child will ever dare to *take*
Somebody's nap again."

CAMP WONDERFUL

I'm going to Camp Wonderful
Beside Lake Paradise
Across from Blissful Mountain
In the Valley of the Nice.
They say it's sunny, cool, and green,
They say the angels made it.
The motto is "Be Fair and Care."
I know I'm gonna *hate* it.

QUALITY TIME

My father is a golfer—
He lets me be his tee.
He puts the ball upon my nose
And hits it right off me.
He says that I can share the joy
Of every ball he hits.
Oh, ain't it grand to have a dad
Who spends time with his kids.

THE FOLKS INSIDE

Inside you, boy,
There's an old man sleepin',
Dreamin', waitin' for his chance.
Inside you, girl,
There's an old lady dozin',
Wantin' to show you a slower dance.

So keep on playin',
Keep on runnin',
Keep on jumpin', 'til the day
That those old folks
Down inside you
Wake up . . . and come out to play.

KEEP-OUT HOUSE

At last—I finished my keep-out house,
A house that's meant for privacy,
A house that's meant for peacefulness,
A house just meant for only me.
There is no door where strangers knock,
No window where they peek and grin.
A perfect private keep-*out* house . . .
Now . . . how do I get in?

HELP!

I walked through the wildwood, and what did I see
But a unicorn with his horn stuck in a tree,
Cryin', "Someone please help me before it's too late."
I hollered, *"I'll* free you." He hollered back, *"Wait—*
How much will it hurt? How long will it take?
Are you sure that my horn will not scratch, bend, or break?
How hard will you pull? How much must I pay?
Must you do it right now or is Wednesday okay?
Have you done this before? Do you have the right tools?
Have you graduated from horn-savin' school?
Will I owe you a favor? And what will it be?
Do you promise that you will not damage the tree?
Should I close my eyes? Should I sit down or stand?
Do you have insurance? Have you washed your hands?
And *after* you free me—tell me what then?
Can you guarantee I won't get stuck *again*?
Tell me *when.* Tell me *how.*
Tell me *why.* Tell me *where.* . . ."

I guess that he's still sittin' there.

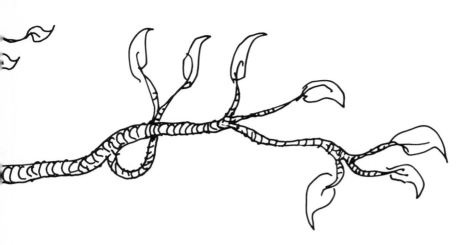

THE SACK RACE

Yes, it's time for the sack race.
Yes, I'm ready to go.
Yes, it's my *first* sack race.
How did you know . . . ?

THREE STINGS

George got stung by a bee and said,
"I wouldn't have got stung if I'd stayed in bed."
Fred got stung and we heard him roar,
"What am I being punished for?"
Lew got stung and we heard him say,
"I learned somethin' about bees today."

EGGS RATED

These eggs
Are eggscellent.
I'm not eggsaggerating.
You can tell by my eggspression
They're eggceptional—
Eggstra fluffy,
Eggstremely tasty,
Cooked eggsactly right
By an eggspert
With lots of eggsperience.
Now I'll eggsamine the bill. . . .
Ooh—much more eggspensive
Than I eggspected.
I gotta get out of here.
Where's the *eggxit*?

YUCK

I stepped in something yucky
As I walked by the crick.
I grabbed a stick to scrape it off,
The yuck stuck to my stick.
I tried to pull it off the stick,
The yuck stuck to my hand.
I tried to wash it off—but it
Stuck to the washin' pan.
I called my dog to pull me loose,
The yuck stuck to his fur.
He rubbed himself against the cat,
The yuck got stuck to her.
My friends and neighbors came to help—
Now all of us are stuck,
Which goes to show what happens
When one person steps in yuck.

CLEAN GENE

Clean Gene is *really* clean—
He is a bath fanatic.
He has six washstands in his room
And twelve tubs in his attic.
He'll wash before he goes to school,
He'll rinse when he gets there.
At recess you can find him
Rubbin' shampoo in his hair.
He buys each new deodorant
To keep him smelling sweet,
He hires a manicurist
For each toenail on his feet.
He only will play baseball
With a Q-tip in each hand,
In case his ears get gritty
From the winds and blowin' sand.
He wears a plastic bubble
So no germs can touch his shirt.
He will not eat potatoes
'Cause potatoes grow in dirt.

He carries toothpaste, and he'll brush
And floss with zest and zeal
Before—and after—and (I'm sorry)
During every meal.
He has a shower above his bed
To spray a soapy stream
(Just in case he ever should
Get dirty in his dreams).
He's hired a man named Henry Grunge,
And when he goes to play,
Grunge runs beside him with a sponge
To wipe his sweat away.
He's built a special music tub
That he can sit right in
'Longside his music teacher
While he plays the violin.
So when you go to visit Gene
Just make sure your jeans are clean,
Just make sure your nails are scrubbed,
Make sure you bring along your tub,
And leave your shoes out in the hall—
If you visit Gene at all.

TELL ME

Tell me I'm clever,
Tell me I'm kind,
Tell me I'm talented,
Tell me I'm cute,
Tell me I'm sensitive,
Graceful and wise,
Tell me I'm perfect—
But tell me the *truth*.

A USE FOR A MOOSE

The antlers of a standing moose,
As everybody knows,
Are just the perfect place to hang
Your wet and drippy clothes.
It's quick and cheap, but I must say
I've lost a lot of clothes that way.

SOMETHIN' NEW

They say, "Come up with somethin' new
And everyone will buy it."
So I came up with a paper umbrella,
But no one was willing to try it.

And then I came up with reusuable gum.
It seemed such a pity to waste it.
Then I came up with some mustard ice cream.
Nobody bothered to taste it.

So now I've invented a plug-bottom boat.
It's just what you need, there's no doubt,
'Cause if any water should ever splash in,
Just pull the plug—it'll all run out.

MOLLY'S FOLLY

Jolly Molly
Went to Bali,
Bought a skateboard,
Tried an Ollie.
Lost her hat,
Dropped her dolly,
Landed *splat*
Right on her collie.
Collie yelled,
"You're off your trolley!"
He bit Molly on her lolly—
That's why Molly
Isn't jolly,
By golly!

THE SMILE MAKERS

The grungy, grumpy, grouchy Giant
Grew tired of his frowny pout
And hired me and Lee to lift
The corners of his crumblin' mouth.
That was last year—and we've been here
Sweatin', strainin' all the while.
Sometimes it sure can be hard work
To make somebody smile.

WHEN I WAS YOUR AGE

My uncle said, "How do you get to school?"
I said, "By bus," and my uncle smiled.
"When I was your age," my uncle said,
"I walked it *barefoot—seven miles.*"

My uncle said, "How much weight can you tote?"
I said, "One bag of grain." My uncle laughed.
"When I was your age," my uncle said,
"I could drive a wagon—and lift a ca*lf.*"

My uncle said, "How many fights have you had?"
I said, "Two—and both times I got whipped."
"When I was your age," my uncle said,
"I fought every day—and was *never* licked."

My uncle said, "How old are you?"
I said, "Nine and a half," and then
My uncle puffed out his chest and said,
"When I was your age . . . I was *ten.*"

BODY LANGUAGE

Said my feet, "Hey, let's go dancin'."
Said my tongue, "Let's have a snack."
Said my brain, "Let's read a good book."
Said my eyes, "Let's take a nap."
Said my legs, "Let's just go walkin'."
Said my back, "Let's take a ride."
Said my seat, "Well, I'll just sit right here,
'Til all of you decide."

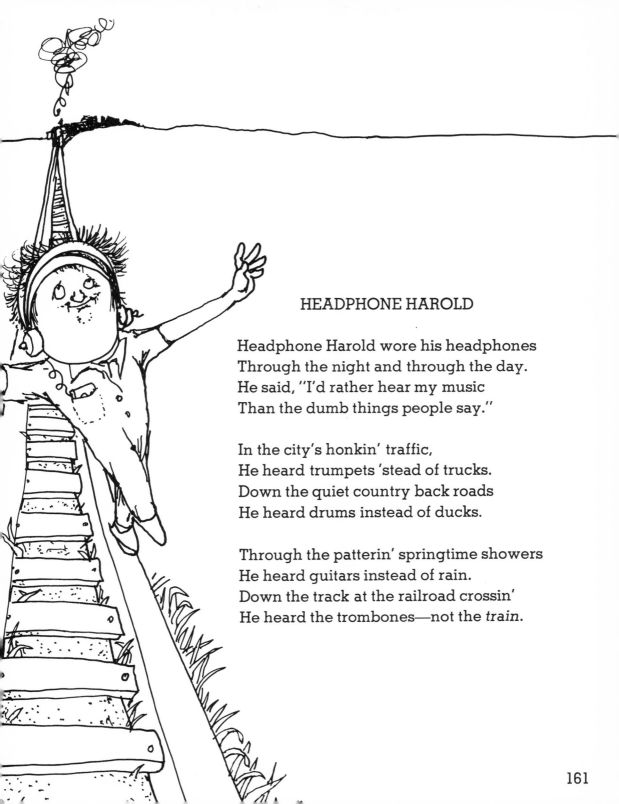

HEADPHONE HAROLD

Headphone Harold wore his headphones
Through the night and through the day.
He said, "I'd rather hear my music
Than the dumb things people say."

In the city's honkin' traffic,
He heard trumpets 'stead of trucks.
Down the quiet country back roads
He heard drums instead of ducks.

Through the patterin' springtime showers
He heard guitars instead of rain.
Down the track at the railroad crossin'
He heard the trombones—not the *train*.

THE FORMER FOREMAN'S STORY

We had to demolish the Johnsons' old house.
I brought in the bulldozers, shovels, and cranes.
We tore off the shingles, we banged in the walls,
We knocked down the chimney, we tore up the drains,
We smashed in the windows, we ripped out the bell,
We cut down the rafters, we sawed up the floor,
We dug up the basement—then somebody yelled,
"Hey, the Johnsons don't live there—they live next door."
(Maybe that's the reason I'm not foreman anymore.)

HUNGRY KID ISLAND

Oh, I'm goin' to Hungry Kid Island,
Way out in the shimmerin' sea.
There's probably hungry kids out there
Who'll share my lunch with me.

But why call it Hungry Kid Island?
There's no kids around that I see,
So I'm goin' to Hungry Kid Island
To solve this mystery.

STORK STORY

You know the stork brings babies,
But did you also know
He comes and gets the older folks
When it's their time to go?

Zooms right down and scoops them up,
Then flaps back out the door
And flies them to the factory where
They all were made before.

And there their skin is tightened up,
Their muscles all are toned,
Their wrinkles all are ironed out,
They're given brand-new bones.

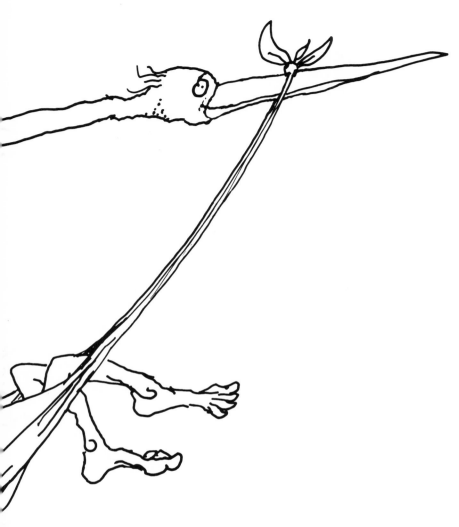

Ol' bent backs are straightened up,
New teeth are added too,
Tired hearts are all repaired
And made to work like new.

Their memories are all removed
And they're shrunk down, and then
The stork flies them back down to earth
As newborn babes again.

CRAZY DREAM

Last night I had a crazy dream
That I was teachin' school.
My teachers had turned into kids,
And I laid down the rules.

I gave 'em a hundred hist'ry books
To memorize each night,
And made 'em read 'em on their heads
Without turnin' on the light.

I sent 'em on a field trip
To the outskirts of Mongolia,
And gave 'em an overnight assignment
To grow a twenty-foot purple magnolia.

I asked 'em how many awful grades
Can cause how many tears?
And if they got one answer wrong,
I just hung 'em up by their ears.

And when they talked or laughed in class,
I pinched 'em 'til they cried
Louder and louder—'til I woke up
Feelin' very satisfied.

41,001² ⟌6,345,596,734.19 ?
WHY DID GEORGE CHERRY CUT DOWN THE WASHINGTON TREE?
NAME OF THE
UT OF THE
STATES?
IF YOU HAD SEVEN APPLES AND YOU GAVE ME THREE, HOW MANY TEETH WOULD A CANARY HAVE?
OSAUR?
CHICKEN?
$11^2 \times 72^3 - 14 = ?$
SO WHAT?
AT IS THE CAPITAL MANGOZENOPIA?
DOES
ANT WEIGH?
142
-143
MIDDLE NAMES
WHO INVENTED THE ROOBISKANKER?
TRANSLATE THE DICTIONARY INTO PIG LATIN
HOW MUCH DOES A SMALL ELEPHANT WEIGH?
LIST 1001 WAYS A MEASLE IS DIFFERENT THAN A WEASEL.
IF YOU HA
IF A
WHO WAS
WHEN DID
IF A
WHERE IS
OW CAN
HY DID
HO FIR
W WILL
CAN A
WHY
IF YOU
RECITE THE ALPHABET... BACKWARD... IN FRENCH... SKIPPING EVERY OTHER LETTER
WHEN WO
OVERBOA
IT?
WILL IT B
PROOVE IT!
GOVIA?
AMIA?
MOBILE?
EED?
WHERE?
WHEN?
WHY?
WHAT HAPPENED IN 1723?.. IN THE AFTERNOON?
COAGULATE THE VERB EECH

IN THE LAND OF . . .

In the land of Listentoemholler
Steaks cost a nickel but the tax is a dollar.
How'd you like to live in Listentoemholler?

In the land of Wailinanweepin'
You work for free and get paid for sleepin'.
How'd you like to live in Wailinanweepin'?

In the land of Ragsanpatches
The men have babies and the ladies have mustaches.
How'd you like to live in Ragsanpatches?

In the land of Muglywugly
You get to be a movie star if you're ugly
And your nose is knobby and your eyes are bugly
And your neck is snugly and your arms are hugly.
Let's all go live in Muglywugly.

THE CASTLE

It's the fabulous castle of *Now*.
You can walk in and wander about,
But it's so very thin,
Once you are, then you've *been*—
And soon as you're in, you're *out*.

INDEX

ONE MORE TIME

For all their patience and loving care in making
this book as good as possible, my deepest thanks
to Joan Robins, Robert Warren, Patty Aitken,
George Craig, and Kim Llewellyn.

And to the picking committee—
Sarah, Matt, Peg, Barbara, Herb, Rebecca, Sam,
and Edite.

Thank you all.

THE END OF THE BOOK—
NO USE TO LOOK
FOR ANY MORE, MY DEAR,
'CAUSE IF YOU TRY FINDING
SOME MORE IN THE BINDING,
YOU MAY JUST...DISAPPEAR

BYE-BYE

S.S.